Smashups

Robert Reed

Jason.
Merry Christmas '06
I am suprised none of your
smash ups are in here!
All the best

Mark.

Schiffer Publishing Ltd

4880 Lower Valley Road, Atglen, PA 19310 USA

Published by Schiffer Publishing Ltd.
4880 Lower Valley Road
Atglen, PA 19310
Phone: (610) 593-1777; Fax: (610) 593-2002
E-mail: Schifferbk@aol.com
Please visit our web site catalog at **www.schifferbooks.com**

This book may be purchased from the publisher.
Include $3.95 for shipping.
Please try your bookstore first.
We are interested in hearing from authors
with book ideas on related subjects.
You may write for a free catalog.

In Europe, Schiffer books are distributed by
Bushwood Books
6 Marksbury Rd.
Kew Gardens
Surrey TW9 4JF England
Phone: 44 (0)181 392-8585; Fax: 44 (0)181 392-9876
E-mail: Bushwd@aol.com

ACKNOWLEDGMENTS

I am grateful to many people who helped me with *Smashups*. David Hofeling of the Naval Institute's photo library in Annapolis, Maryland, took time out from his busy schedule to help me locate shipwreck images. Sam Daniel at the Prints and Photos Division of the Library of Congress came through with some sources I might otherwise have missed. Ed McCarter of the Still Photos Division at the National Archives patiently helped me through several research problems.

Bob Browning, U.S. Coast Guard Historian, permitted me to use his extensive files. He was always cooperative and friendly.

Ben Kelly, Director of the Insurance Institute for Highway Safety, gave me good advice; moreover, he took me to lunch at the Watergate.

Jack White, railway historian and an old friend, gave me much valuable help with *Smashups*. The late Paul Garber of the National Air Museum shared his collection of air crashes with me. Walter Boyne, aviation writer, helped me to identify the planes in my air crash photos.

Irene Jackson, public relations person with Japan Airlines in New York, was astonishingly forthcoming and efficient in answering my questions.

Photographer and friend Louise Kraft gave me her trained eye by pointing out some of the subtle differences between good black and white prints and excellent ones. She knew what to look for when I didn't.

Carolyn Smith, photo librarian at the National Red Cross Headquarters, kindly located some fine images for my collection.

Irwin Garrett, photo journalist from Faquier County, Virginia, permitted me to use several of his auto wreck photographs.

My publisher, Peter Schiffer, encouraged me to resume work on *Smashups* after a long hiatus. He always gave me encouragement. When I was anxious and obsessive about a missed deadline, he eased my worries by reminding me that a project like *Smashups* should be enjoyable. And that if it is not, one would be better advised to read books, not write them. Without Peter my work would still be moldering in my attic.

INTRODUCTION

Life is a misadventure. Yesterday morning, I barked my shin in the tool shed, drawing blood. An hour later, I stepped off the wrong rung on a step ladder and jarred my back teeth upon hitting the ground. In the afternoon, I drove over a curb in Winchester, causing my foot to slip off the clutch and the truck to buck like a stag in rut, the tires to squeal, and the engine to die. I felt like an idiot. These were just few of the day's accidents. Such mishaps are ordinary occurrences for all of us. Then there are the larger accidents.

Recently, public radio out of Washington, D.C., reported that a high speed passenger train traveling between Munich and Hanover, Germany, had derailed at 120 miles an hour, smashing the engine and a dozen coaches. Public radio and its affiliate stations throughout America repeated the story every half hour throughout the morning and afternoon. CNN picked up the story and showed video clips of the wreck scene. So did ABC, CBS, FOX, and NBC during their evening news coverage. We're talking about a train wreck in Germany, for goodness sake.

Train wrecks are still big news, even though almost no one travels by train anymore. But wrecks are photogenic and they make good copy.

Plane wrecks can be huge news and ship wrecks, too, especially cruise ships. Car wrecks make big local news. Sometimes they become national or even international news. Wreck photos are intriguing. Wrecks of all sorts are indispensable to CNN and the daily press.

A jetliner goes down in the Atlantic off Nova Scotia. An Amtrak train derails and fouls the East coast Mainline. A tractor trailer hauling a cargo of live chickens jackknifs and rolls over on the Washington, D.C., beltway during morning rush hour. A ferry with three hundred passengers sinks in a monsoon in Bangladesh. Such stories attract media attention nearly every day.

Why all this fascination with vehicle accidents, which often lead to despair, injury, and even death?

Learning of or witnessing a serious accident is at first a vicarious scare accompanied by the thrill of danger. Often what follows are feelings of relief and safety, because the accident didn't happen to us. Wasn't that plane crash terrible? Thank goodness it didn't happen to us. We escaped harm's way. That feeling is called *shadenfreude*, the good feeling we experience when bad things happen to other people.

When I wrote *Train Wrecks* several years ago, I remember that one prospective publisher rejected the proposal because he thought the idea lugubrious and would repel readers. He was off base. The book was published, has remained in print for many years, and sold well enough to make me happy.

I now offer you *Smashups: The Hazard of Travel* an iconography of travel accidents of all genres—air, highway, railway, and water—involving trucks, buses, cars, light planes, jetliners, seaplanes, freight trains, ship wrecks aplenty, European wrecks, Asian wrecks, American wrecks, minor crashes, major ones, horse and cart wrecks, freak accidents, and even ordinary ones.

This iconography represents a search of fifteen years. Most of the photographs have never been published before in America. Thanks to *Smashups* you can read through the pictures and experience the thrill of danger in the safety of your own home.

I hope you find these misadventures interesting.

Robert Reed
Alexandria, Virginia

Right: A low slung Mercury tangled with an Army truck at 17th and Potomac Avenue, near the Washington Monument in Washington, D.C., September 2, 1950. *Bureau of Public Roads.*

The coastal trawler *O.M. Arnold* ran onto the Butterworth Rocks off South Dundar Island, British Columbia. Date Unknown. *Wisconsin State Historical Society.*

Norfolk & Western's new streamliner lies on its side after running off the rails at a bad curve. The weight of the fallen locomotive buckled the parallel tracks. Powhatan, West Virginia, June 12, 1941. *Library of Congress.*

When the driver, Dan Alsop, attempted to stop his Hoosier Highways truck on a slippery winter morning, his semi jackknifed and rolled over with the cab cocked skyward. St. Louis, Missouri, February 11, 1936. *St. Louis Dispatch.*

This smashup took place when the driver of a heavy dump truck attempted to make a sharp left turn in front of a tram on Rue Victor Hugo. Brussels, Belgium, May 20, 1949. *New York Times.*

When the Panama Ltd. derailed near Batesville, Mississippi, November 11, 1937, a combination baggage car/club car carrying fifteen thoroughbred race horses was thrown off the track. The car landed, jutting sharply in the air. A local newspaper reported that the accident was caused by a cow and her calf, which had strayed from their pasture onto the track. Is this explanation credible? *National Archives.*

Illinois Central Railroad's City of Miami lies jackknifed and sprawling over the tracks. Spring rains had partially washed out the trackbed. Champaign, Illinois, April 20, 1947. *Chicago Historical Society.*

This big 6-engine French flying-boat made an Atlantic tour in 1935. While anchored in Pensacola Bay, Florida, high winds caused the craft to go airborne at its mooring and flip over. The plane in this view is being salvaged from the bay so that it may be returned to France. This plane was one of the largest of its time, capable of carrying 170 people. *National Archives.*

An amphibious Consolidated PBY nosed off the parking strip when the brakes failed. Amchitaka, Alaska, June 26, 1943. *U.S. Navy.*

5

The Toulouse-Condom
motorbus didn't stop quite
in time and hit a branch-line
steam locomotive at a grade
crossing. Near Auch,
France, June 1, 1934. Much
hands on hip body language.
Author's Collection.

To avoid hitting an abandoned car on the bridge over the Nansemond River near Churchland, Virginia, the driver skidded this Greyhound bus on the icy roadway and bashed through the bridge railing. February 21, 1950. *Richmond Times*.

The Korean cargo vessel *Chil Bosan 6* with 100,000 gallons of diesel fuel broke a propeller shaft and drifted into the Alaskan coast. The Bearing Sea, February, 1985. *The Naval Institute.*

The freighter *Mohawk* lost power and was blown ashore near Annapolis, Maryland, in September of 1978. She rests against the piers of the Chesapeake Bay Bridge. *Maryland Historical Society.*

A seriously wrecked Mercury convertible. I believe the vernacular is "totaled." The driver hit a tree near Princeton, New Jersey, on September 14, 1947. *Bureau of Public Roads.*

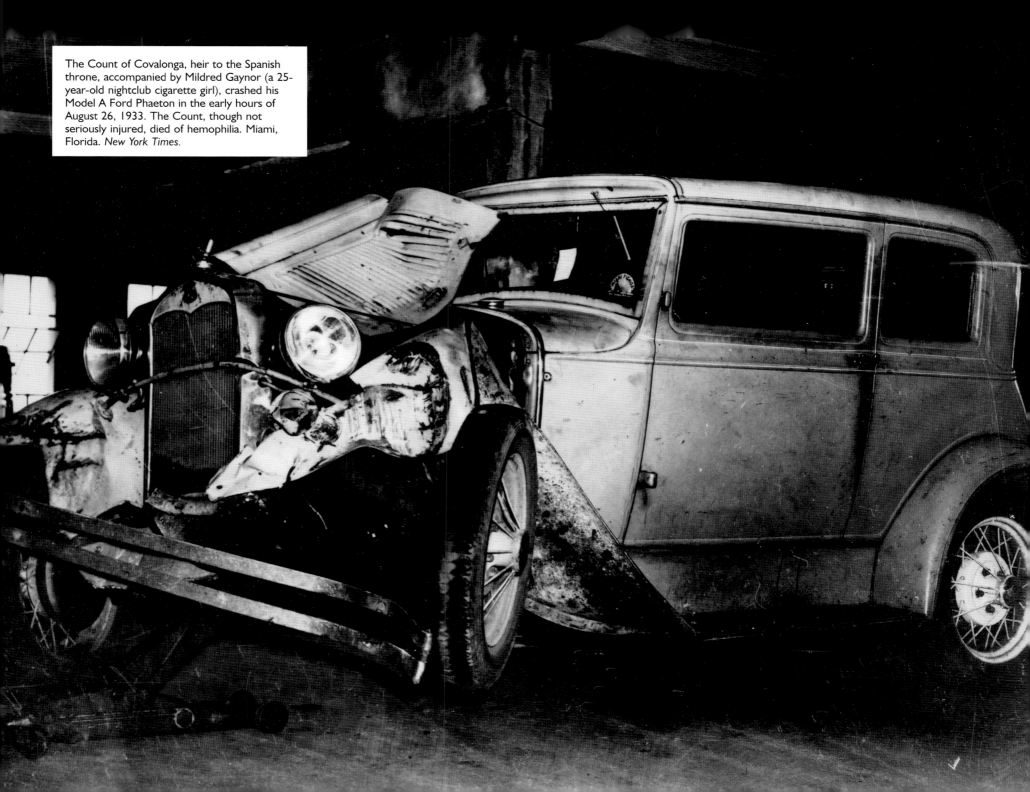

The Count of Covalonga, heir to the Spanish throne, accompanied by Mildred Gaynor (a 25-year-old nightclub cigarette girl), crashed his Model A Ford Phaeton in the early hours of August 26, 1933. The Count, though not seriously injured, died of hemophilia. Miami, Florida. *New York Times*.

When the engine failed, the pilot of this Navy Hellcat found a muddy swamp and slid to safety at Daytona Beach, Florida, on December 5, 1944. *U.S. Navy.*

When the landing gear didn't engage, the pilot of this Boeing B-17 Flying Fortress made a safe crash landing near Dallas, Texas, on November 11, 1942. Thirteen thousand of these big bombers were built for World War II service. *National Archives.*

The Canadian Pacific liner *Princess Kathleen*, on the final voyage of the season from Vancouver, B.C., to Skagway, Alaska, steamed onto a high ledge of rock on the Alaskan mainland on September 7, 1952, with 425 passengers and crew aboard. A thick slash had been torn in the ship's hull from bow to midships. Passengers are being taken aboard a Coast Guard cutter. *Chicago Historical Society.*

As crewmen watch, the Scot-built liner *Princess Kathleen* slipped off the reef and sank stern first then heeled over and sank in 33 fathoms. *Chicago Historical Society.*

Running under strict black-out regulations imposed by the British government during World War II, the LMS Night Scot ran smack into a switch engine just in front of the station platform at Bletchey. The impact threw the switch engine into the dining room of the station. It was a nightmare of tea urns and scones. Buckinghamshire, England, October 14, 1939. *New York Times.*

A New York bound Central Railroad of New Jersey passenger train carrying 300 conventioneers smacked into a Buick stalled on the track south of Philadelphia. Several cars were tossed off the elevated track by the sudden impact. Date Unknown. *Author's Collection.*

The Boston & Albany railroad bridge at Chester, Massachusetts, collapsed in 1907, sending the locomotive and six coaches into a rocky stream bed. *Author's Collection.*

At the height of wartime traffic, on December 14, 1943, a B & O locomotive derailed in the Baltimore tunnel near Camden station, snarling traffic for hours. *Maryland Historical Society.*

Norwegian merchant ship *Granville* lists sharply and sinks rapidly after running onto rocks and ripping her bottom plates. The accident happened at the entrance to Vancouver, British Columbia, harbor on a stormy morning in January, 1949. *National Archives.*

After a late night tour of nightclubs, the driver of this speeding car went out of control and smashed into a flower shop on Rue de Bonlainvilliers. Paris, France, September 6, 1935. *Author's Collection.*

Just as this Piper was coming in to land at Stinson Municipal Airport, the engine died. The plane first hit a power line then came to rest on the top of a house. Date Unknown. *FAA*

A North American built Navy SNJ chewed into a Stimson trainer, whose propeller was splintered in the collision. Daytona Beach, Florida, June 19, 1943. *National Archives.*

When the motor vessel *State Command* bashed into a Hunt Oil Company drilling platform in the Gulf of Mexico, the ship carried the iron superstructure piggyback, balanced on her bridge back to port. Morgan City, Louisiana, August 21, 1976. *U.S. Naval Academy.*

A river crane begins to remove a National Airlines 727 from its submarine landing field. This is an unidentified FAA photograph. My most reliable authority believed it to be the Potomac River near Reagan National Airport. I could not confirm his report. *FAA*

The boiler of this New York Central locomotive exploded at Bellefontaine, Ohio, on April 25, 1942, exposing the fire box and exhaust. *Lima News.*

The prow of the USS *Guadalupe* was crumpled after she rammed the USS *Nantahala* at Ulithi Lagoon in the Carolina Islands, which lie south of Guam. February, 1945. *U.S. Navy.*

On July 11, 1961, United Air Lines DC-8 passenger jet crashed while landing at Denver, Colorado. Due to failure of the hydraulic system, the pilot could not control the plane on touchdown, and the aircraft ran off the runway several hundred feet. *NSTB (National Transportation Safety Board).*

World Airways DC-10 skidded off the icy runway at Boston's Logan Airport and came to rest on the shore of Boston Harbor. The nose cone snapped off the fuselage of the wide-body jetliner. January 5, 1982. *National Archives.*

A country road accident near Sidney, New York, 1928. A Ford Model T hit a roadside utility pole. *Bureau of Public Roads.*

A messy accident occurred when a light farm truck rear-ended a touring car from Ohio. Near Gaithersburg, Maryland, August 30, 1923. *Bureau of Public Roads*.

An ironically sylvan and serene image taken in Rock Creek Park, Washington, D.C. A Dodge touring car fell into a ravine after running off the Connecticut Avenue Bridge. Father and barefoot lad look at the wreckage. Date unknown. *The Washington Star.*

A solemn crowd surrounds a Model T Ford that skidded into a street lamp pole at 13th and R streets in Northwest Washington, D.C., 1922. All T's were painted black because black enamel was the only paint that would dry quickly enough to keep up with the assembly line. *Library of Congress*.

Workmen struggle to remove a heavy steel plate of the hull of the Liberian oilier *Corinthos* after it was rammed broadside by the U.S. chemical tanker *Edgar M. Queeny*. The *Corinthos* caught fire and exploded, sending this hunk of hull onto the deck of the *Queeny*. The Delaware River at Marcus Hook, Pennsylvania, January 31, 1975. *Philadelphia Inquirer.*

Crewmen huddle in the bow of the sinking British freighter *Ambassador*, which lists steeply in heaving seas. U.S. Coast Guardsmen from the *Coos Bay* stand ready to pull survivors over a lifeline. A heroic rescue. Off the Grand Banks, the North Atlantic, February 19, 1964. *USCG*

This image from the collection of the Air Museum bore no identification. The photograph illustrates how the early aircrafts, such as this Jenny Cub, could roost in trees because of their light weight and slow speed. *Air Museum*.

This 1951 Chevrolet Fleetline 2-door was wrecked when it plowed into a Pontiac near The Plains, Virginia, 1952. The slant-back design was thought to be particularly stylish. *Collection of C.I. Garrett.*

The inevitable crowd gathered to look at the damage of a smashup between a three-wheeled delivery wagon and a truck carrying bags of coal arranged with Teutonic precision. Friedrichstrasse, near the Brandenburg Gate, Berlin, Germany, June 20, 1938. *National Archives*.

A Philadelphia streetcar slipped off the tracks on a curve and bashed into the entrance of Frank's Lunchroom. The motorman was charged with operating at an excessive speed. June 20, 1952. *Library of Congress.*

A locomotive fell into the street and partially destroyed an apartment building after two freight trains smashed head-on at an overpass in the city center. Essen, Germany, May 31, 1931. *Deutche Bundesbahn.*

The Paris to Vienna Express derailed after it struck a milk truck at a grade crossing near the Vaihingen/Enz Station. The impact sent the locomotive on its side across the triple track mainline. Wurttemberg, Germany. Date unknown. *National Archives*.

During a general railway strike in France, saboteurs unbolted 30 meters of track on the mainline between Paris and Fille. On March 12, 1949, a mail train flashed off the track and smashed up seven passenger cars. This image shows a particularly wicked telescope of cars. *French National Rail.*

Left and above: A 1947 Plymouth pulled out from a side road and blindsided a Buick. Near Rectortown, Virginia, 1947. *C.I. Garrett Collection.*

A Hudson and Manhattan tube train crashed into a partly open draw bridge over the Passaic River near Newark, New Jersey, December 17, 1945. Despite their steel construction, two coaches were crushed by the force of the impact. *American Red Cross*.

A turntable overrun at a GER roundhouse at Swaffam, January, 1894. The engine knocked down a buffer stop and fell backward down a hillside into the street. *National Rail Museum, York, UK.*

Lethal rocks caught the schooner
Miapu. She sank by the bows. Hell Bay,
The Isles of Scilly, July 27, 1879. *The
Gibsons.*

The frame was all that remained of this Santa Fe locomotive, which exploded, sending the boiler, fire box, and cab two hundred yards away. The accident occurred near Standish, Missouri, in winter, 1920. *NTSB*

An unusual triple smashup occurred on a snowy morning, January 26, 1936, at the Hatfield, Hertfordshire, England, depot. Three London and Northeastern Railway trains were wrecked. First the morning Cambridge to Kings Cross Express crashed into the back of a stationary fish train. The momentum of the collision pushed the fish train forward into the rear of a stopped passenger train. *British Rail.*

The face of this Southern Pacific diesel unit was charred after it struck a gasoline tank truck at a highway grade crossing at Big Wells, Texas, June 17, 1961. *Smithsonian Institution*.

Left: Rock ledges had to be dynamited before the Grand Trunk Pacific passenger liner *Prince Rupert* could be refloated. She ran ashore on Glenn Island in a gale, en route to Anyox, British Columbia, March 23, 1917. *Seattle Post*.

A rural wooden plank bridge was unable to take the weight of a heavy Federal Six truck, which appears undamaged in the fall near Shawnee, Oklahoma, April, 1927. *Library of Congress*.

A group of men and boys, including two county constables, look at this bizarre scene. A farmer's horse hangs from an old stone bridge in Gloucestershire, England, c.1900. *Library of Congress*.

A US Air 737 crashed on takeoff at La Guardia Airport, New York, on September 20, 1989. The plane bound for Charlotte, North Carolina, overran the runway and crashed into the East River, its body crushed, its nose resting on a pier. *NTSB*.

A New Zealand flying boat tore off a right wing when it crashed into a cargo vessel while landing. Segond Channel, Espiritu Santo, October 31, 1943. *New York Times*.

What did the *Star K* hit? A pier?
Another ship? Whatever, the Jaws
profile is unmistakable. Location and
date unknown. *U.S. Coast Guard.*

A view of the stern section of the tanker *African Queen*, which split in two after she grounded on shore. Derelict, the ship lists, her main deck awash, and her hold filled with a million dollars of crude oil from Columbia. Eleven miles east of Ocean City, Maryland, December 30, 1958. *Baltimore Sun*.

A highway guard rail, rather than protecting a driver, speared into the driver's seat and sliced through the roof. Baltimore, Maryland, 1971. Such accidents brought about a redesign of guard rails. *Baltimore News-American.*

A speeding car ran through the guard rail of the Monroe Street Bridge in Alexandria, Virginia, May 17, 1913, and fell into the Richmond, Fredericksburg, and Potomac railyard. A thrill of danger runs through the crowd. *Bureau of Public Roads*.

A summer road accident in Potomac, Maryland, August, 1950. A Chevrolet overturned when the driver attempted to pass on a curve, ignoring the double line warning. *Bureau of Public Roads.*

A four-engine Avro Tudor, chartered by rugby fans returning from the Belfast matches, came in too low and crashed short of the Llandow Airport. Near Cardiff, Wales, March 12, 1950. *New York Times.*

A Curtis JN4 Jennie biplane made a soft but sudden landing in a newly plowed field a half mile north of Preston Field in Idaho. March 3, 1919. *Air Museum.*

The clipper *Glenbervie* is caught in the Manacles in a heavy sea. A crowd of men and boys hoped to salvage the thousand barrels of whiskey aboard. Near Lowland Point, Cornwall, England, December, 1901. *The Gibsons.*

This handsome engine over ran its buffers on a roundhouse and dropped into a turntable pit. Because the engine was moving at a slow pace, the fall did little damage. Railroad mechanics are jacking up the engine to track level, while the crew from her sister engine 1346 look on. Date Unknown. *National Rail Museum, York, UK.*

Steel construction did not make passenger cars invulnerable to damage. When a freight locomotive sideswiped a stationary mail train bound for Paris, the steel cars were slashed open on impact. The accident occurred in Dijonville, France, April 21, 1937. *Author's Collection*.

When the boiler of an Ulster & Delaware Railroad 10-wheeler locomotive burst on August 23, 1930, the engine flew off the track and landed on her head. *Author's Collection.*

The driver of a dump truck hauling gravel stalled at a grade crossing near Council Bluffs, Iowa. A Burlington passenger train struck the truck, derailed the entire train, and destroyed two diesel locomotives. October 15, 1966. *Author's Collection.*

A Model T four-seater was broadsided and knocked onto the sidewalk in an accident that occurred at Massachusetts Avenue just off Dupont Circle, Washington, D. C. Winter, 1910. *Columbia Historical Society.*

A crazy smash-up between two Dodges and a tree on Wisconsin Avenue in Georgetown, D.C., 1919. By this date, Dodge was second in auto production behind only front-runner Ford. *Author's Collection.*

The driver swerved to avoid hitting a child playing in the street and flipped his Chevrolet onto its roof. Philadelphia, Pennsylvania, September 7, 1930. *University of Pennsylvania.*

A 1941 Chevy clashed with a farm truck on a narrow country road near Zanesville, Ohio, 1947. Note the plaid seat covers, so common in that era. *Author's Collection.*

The Japanese freighter *KoKaKu Maru* staggers to port with a badly damaged hull and bridge after being hit by the Military Sea Transport refrigeration ship *Asterion*. The accident occurred in a fog, thirty miles northwest of San Francisco, California, June 5, 1963. *USCG.*

An overhead view of the *C.E. Dant* (*right*), which bit deeply into the *Agean Sea* in a fog. The Strait of Juan de Fuca, entrance to Puget Sound, Washington, October 4, 1972. *USCG*

The U.S. Steel Corporation's *J.P. Morgan, Jr.*, bound for Pittsburgh with iron ore, collided bows-on with the passenger steamer *Crete* off Devil's Island, Lake Superior. Date Unknown. *Great Lakes Research Center.*

The engine room of the grain hulk *Kirby Smith* was ripped open after being rammed by the Swedish vessel *Nyland*. Hampton roads, Virginia, March 17, 1956. A hulk is a ship used as a storehouse or prison, not for sea service. The Department of Agriculture stores surplus grain in decommissioned Navy ships. *U.S. Navy.*

The bow of the USS *Shaw* was ripped apart after smashing into the very ship she was escorting, the British troopship *Aquitania*. They were practicing zigzag maneuvers. Near Southampton, England, October, 1918. *U.S. Navy.*

The stern section of the American tanker *Pine Ridge* wallows in heavy seas 125 miles east of Cape Hatteras, North Carolina, after the ship split in two on December 21, 1960. The severed stern was towed to Newport News, Virginia, for salvage. *Charlotte Observer*.

The handsome Pullman cars of a Missouri, Kansas, and Texas Railroad passenger train sprawl lazily beside a field. A broken rail derailed the cars, which were moving at a slow speed. San Marco, Texas, September 16, 1914. *Author's Collection*.

The oil laden Greek tanker *Dauntless Colocotronis* gashed her bottom on a sunken barge. Crude oil caught fire and destroyed the ship. The Mississippi River, near New Orleans, Louisiana, July 6, 1972. *Library of Congress.*

DAUNTLESS COLOCOTRONIS

The surprise explosion of the Delaware & Hudson Railroad's new Mallet locomotive caused a dozen boxcars to slue along a hillside near Cobleskill, New York, in 1941. *Author's Collection.*

A DC-3 carrying freight from London to Leeds, England, had difficulty gaining altitude during its take off in a snow storm.
It smashed into the roof of an unoccupied house while holding an admirably level fight. Date unknown. *Air Museum.*

The original caption of the news photograph of this freakish accident stated that a coal car had jumped the track and landed atop of this Chevy. Or is this an illusion? Bryn Mawr, Pennsylvania, December 12, 1930. *Author's Collection.*

A yellow Oldsmobile 98 Convertible traveling at high speed on a Saturday night skidded off the road on a curve and smashed into a tree broadside. Hattiesburg, Mississippi, February 19, 1950. *Atlanta Journal*.

The Bristol Scout 4675 landed heavily, cracked its nose, and flipped over on a grassy field. Date and location unknown.
Air Museum.

A spring rain storm flipped this US Army Babcock glider at Deland, Florida, March 2, 1945. Note the tears in the fabric skin of the plane. *National Archives*.

A passenger locomotive, overturned and still breathing steam, has drawn a crowd of curious spectators. Pittsburgh, Pennsylvania, May 15, 1902. *Author's Collection.*

Just south of Washington, D.C., in Virginia, Southern Railway's crack Crescent Ltd., traveling from New York City to New Orleans, slipped off the track at a bridge weakened by heavy autumn rains. The locomotive plowed into a mudbank. Several coaches jackknifed and tumbled into each other in a messy pile up of steel. The locomotive burrowed into the riverbank. *Richmond Times Dispatch.*

In the shadow of the Williamsburgh Bridge, the bow of the American tanker *Empress Bay* slowly sinks in the East River after a fiery collision with the Swedish freighter *Nebraska*. The tanker's 280,000 gallons of gasoline spewed into the river, ignited, and endangered the Manhattan and Brooklyn waterfronts. New York City, June 25, 1958. *USCG.*

The center span of the Benjamin Harrison Memorial Bridge collapsed into the James River after the S.S. *Marine Floridian* struck a pier. Hopewell, Virginia, February 24, 1977. *Naval Institute*.

An ironic wreck on L'avenue de la Defense in Courbevoie, France, February 26, 1939. The car hit a stop light. Pedestrians appear to enjoy a diversion from the bleak mid-winter of northern France. *National Archives.*

A Renault limo belonging to the Mayor crashed into a lamppost on a boulevard in Nice, France. Date unknown. *Embassy of France.*

A Long Island Railroad locomotive rammed the rear of a stalled freight, smashing two wooden box cars to splinters. Bay Shore, Long Island, July 10, 1909. *Library of Congress.*

Steam hoists clear the wreckage of the B & O Railroad's Diplomat, which rear ended a freight train in the mountains of West Virginia near Newburg, November 18, 1946. *Smithsonian Institution*.

The engine stopped just in time. A big Santa Fe Alco diesel-electric locomotive had brake failure as it approached the Los Angeles depot. The train charged through the buffers, sped on through the parking lot, and stopped. Suspended fifteen feet above the street, literally the locomotive is hanging by a thread—in this case an electric power line. January 28, 1948. *NTSB-National Transportation Safety Board.*

The heavy Atlantic waves pound the British tanker *Clam* (owned by the Anglo-Saxon Petroleum Company), which is caught on the rocks near Reykjanes, Iceland. The ship was being towed to Cardiff, Wales, for repairs when the towline broke and the ship was swept into the rocky coast. March 6, 1955. *New York Times*.

Icy road conditions sent this school bus off a country road and into a tree. Then a Plymouth, unable to stop, smacked into it near Ft. Wayne, Indiana, 1945. *Author's Collection*.

Wintry weather conditions and poor visibility contributed to a smashup between a Dodge and a semi near Muncie, Indiana, February, 1946. *Author's Collection.*

On March 18, 1912, a locomotive undergoing repair at the Southern Pacific shops at San Antonio, Texas, exploded with terrific force. One chunk of the boiler weighing 16,000 pounds was blown 1,200 feet and smashed into a nearby boarding house. *Author's Collection.*

On Saturday morning, June 12, 1882, a seven-car Hartford-bound passenger train carrying Connecticut farm families to the city fell through a wooden bridge over Camp Creek. A heavy spring rain the day before had weakened the bridge. *Author's Collection.*

The square-rigged *Eira* ran onto rocks during an arctic exploration voyage. For extra caution she also carries a steam engine. Alaska, c.1880. *Naval Historical Center.*

Two Scottish Motor Transport motor coaches collided at Kepperock Corner at the foot of Lylestone Brae when the double-decker skidded on a greasy road. October 20, 1936. *Collection of Thomas Skinner, Edinburgh, Scotland.*

Pilot Illwood and engineer Guilford stand happily beside the British test-plane *Concordia* at Bromma Airport, Stockholm, Sweden. The test plane made a crash landing without the nose wheel engaged. While the plane circled the field for a hour to empty the fuel tanks, the British Ambassador, Sir Bertrand Jerram, arrived at the airport to treat the heroic crew to a drink when they landed. October 30, 1935. *British Embassy.*

A Lockheed Ventura landing at South Weymouth, Massachusetts, over ran the tarmac and fell into a rocky field. September, 1944. *U.S. Photographic Center.*

A wreckage of splintered wooden freight cars and crumpled locomotives piled up after two freight trains of the Southern Railway crashed head-on. Hither Green, England, May 9, 1934. *British Rail.*

A B-25 medium bomber *Mitchell* suffered considerable damage when it was dropped on the dock by a careless crane operator at Pearl Harbor, Hawaii, January 11, 1944. *National Archives*.

A Royal Dutch Shell tanker truck carrying twenty tons of heating oil hit a lamp post, swerved away, and overturned in Garrett Lane in Wandsworth, England, March 18, 1931. Two drivers were taken into custody for public endangerment. *New York Times*.

A locomotive pokes out from the show window of a candy store. How did this accident happen? Date and location unknown. *Allen County Historical Society, Lima, Ohio.*

A 1934 Ford clipped a utility pole on U.S. Route 1 in Alexandria, Virginia, in April of 1938. *Bureau of Public Roads.*

In a crazy triple crash, one car finished upside down on top of two others. The smashup occurred on the Kingston by-pass near Esher, England, on July 16, 1939. *London Times.*

The Alaska Steamship Company's finest liner *Mariposa* ran ashore in a fog at Sumner Strait, Alaska, on October 8, 1915. *Seattle Historical Society.*

Right: The pilot of a JAL flight from Tokyo, coming in on visual on a foggy day, landed too early and went down in shallow water in San Francisco Bay on November 22, 1968. *Japan Air Lines.*

Left: A view of New York Central's Mercury observation car after it was rammed by the Commodore Vanderbilt near Rockey Ridge, Ohio, in 1938. The Vanderbilt's engineer tried to avoid the collision by slamming on the brakes. However, the brakes failed to hold on the slippery rails. *Cleveland Plain Dealer.*

Right: As a result of a switching error and an abrupt stop, these old wooden freight cars buckled at a bizarre angle. The trucks of the car on the right were left on the track. Gare de Longjumeau, Paris, France, April 4, 1937. *French National Rail.*

The U.S. Coast Guard brings survivors ashore with a breeches buoy from the stranded schooner *W.N. Reinhardt* out of Barbados. Nantucket, June 8, 1927. *USCG.*

Right: A destructive gale in the North Atlantic split the hull of the British freighter *Somerset Woods*. She sank off the coast of St. Johns, Newfoundland, Canada. Date unknown. *The Naval Institute.*

The L.A.P.D. assists in removing a wrecked Plymouth from the San Bernadino Freeway, 1955. Poor highway design caused the accident. The driver, veering right to the exit ramp, crashed into a steel pole that held a traffic direction sign. *National Highway Users Association.*

This smashup is the result of the driver's failing to observe a stop sign. Local residents attempt to right the overturned Mercury. Near Oxford, Mississippi, 1951. *Insurance Institute for Highway Safety.*

The railing was not strong enough. A Chevy burst through the old guardrail and dandled nervously over the Mississippi River. Minneapolis, Minnesota, February 20, 1932. *Milwaukee Historic Society.*

After a forced landing in a residential neighborhood in Sayville, New York, pilot Dow Waters of Mineola, New York, escaped injury. His light plane ended the early morning flight in this odd position. February 19, 1951. Note the lineman cutting off the power. *New York Times*.

The cargo ship *Puerto Rican*, loaded with incompatible chemicals, exploded and broke in two. The stern section wallowed helplessly in the calm seas for two days before sinking. The Pacific Ocean, October 31, 1984. *Library of Congress.*

The crew of the Plymouth fishing trawler *Reginald* take their tea on the rocks where the ship ran aground. On the next high tide, they floated her off. Near St. Mary's, The Isles of Scilly, Cornwall, England, 1902. *The Gibsons*.

The driver of a motor-wagon belonging to an urgent dispatch company was hurrying to deliver legal documents when he ran off the road into Marianne Graf's apparel shop in Vienna, Austria. The street sweeper has already shown up for duty. What tidy people, those Austrians. Date Unknown. *New York Times*.

The driver of a Boston, Massachusetts, taxicab smashed through the railings of a shop on West Newton Streett and took a nosedive into the basement entrance of a printing shop below George Sing's laundry and the Deelight Deli. Is that George smiling? May 12, 1931. *Boston Public Library.*

A morning commuter train headed for Tokarozawa rammed into the rear of a freight train on a single track. Several coaches were telescoped by the impact. Rescue workers search through the wreckage. Tokyo, Japan, January 21, 1940. *Author's Collection.*

A train carrying laborers from the Wasserling Valley sped out of control, smashed through the buffers, dashed into the train shed, and bashed into the wall of the station. Mulhouse, Alsace, France, near the German border, June 22, 1934. *National Archives.*

A Ford coupe ran off the road and skidded broadside into a cedar tree. Instant demolition. Delaplane, Virginia, 1950.
C.I. Garrett Collection.

A spring twister toppled a large elm tree onto a grocer's delivery truck. Note the missing wall on the house to the left. Cape Giardeau, Missouri, May 21, 1949. *American Red Cross.*

The American passenger steamer *Pilgrim* ran onto a rocky shelf at Chebeague Island, Maine, on July 7, 1929. What a remarkable state of balance. *Library of Congress.*

The Swedish freighter *Nyland* injured her prow after slicing the *Kirby Smith* nearly in half. The *Kirby Smith* was a grain storage vessel at anchor. Hampton Roads, Virginia, March 17, 1956. *U.S. Navy.*

Below: A limousine owned by the Comte de Montpelier ran onto a rocky Atlantic coast at St. Nazaire-Trignac, France, on July 21, 1937. *Author's Collection*.

Right: A scene of happy confusion. Everyone in the crowd is smiling about the amusing clash of two Washington, D.C., trolley cars and a Ford towncar, May 6, 1925. That's springtime. *Smithsonian Institution*.

A stolen Pontiac dandles precariously over a construction trench after fleeing car thieves crashed through a barricade in their flight. New York City, December 30, 1946. *New York Times*.

A Beech C45, flown by a student pilot, landed a bit off-course on the roof of an apartment building in Romainville, France, on January 26, 1948. *French National Rail.*

Race car driver J.B. Marquis lost control of his Sunbeam at a curve in the Santa Monica, California, road race, in 1914.
Author's Collection.

An Overland touring car ran into a tree stump hidden by weeds and broke an axle two miles from Waterboro, South Carolina, on July 14, 1910. The headlights bounced off from the impact. *University of South Carolina.*

Naval investigators seem to be having a good time looking over a Marine B-25 bomber that landed in shallow water near Key West, Florida, in February, 1944. *National Archives*.

A New England Air Express charter flight made an emergency landing on the beach of Eleuthera. When food supplies were depleted, the stranded passengers etched a sign on the sand. The Bahamas, British West Indies, October 5, 1948. *New York Times.*

Swerving to avoid hitting a pedestrian crossing Regent Street, an elegant British firetruck rammed into a fireplug. I believe it's called irony. Trafalgar Square, London, England, April 4, 1936. *British Tourist Office*.

It happened in front of the Rennes Auto School. An empty cattle truck traveling along Avenue d'Orleans tailgated a Ford, then bashed into the base of a statue commemorating pharmacists Pelletier and Ventou. Paris, France. Date unknown. *Library of Congress*.

The driver had jumped to safety just before a B & O steam locomotive destroyed his coupe at a grade crossing in Branchville, Maryland, November, 1936. *Bureau of Public Roads.*

Because of a brakeman's negligence, a string of thirty-six petrol cisterns (British for oil tank cars) ran away downgrade, piling up and tumbling into each other when they tipped off the rails and fell into a row of houses. Fortunately, the cisterns were empty. Constantza, Romania. Date unknown. *National Archives*.

The USS *Lafayette* caught fire and perished in her berth in the New York Harbor while she was being converted into a troopship. The U.S. Navy confiscated the ship as a war prize when the French government was controlled by the Germans during World War II. She had earlier been the French luxury liner *Normandie*, an Air Deco masterpiece. February 9, 1942. *U.S. Navy.*

A Sudden Plunge
- yet -
An undamaged "For[d]"
© BY-W.D. OFF. 8/3[1]

A shining new Ford-T went off the road into a culvert in rural Oklahoma on August 31, 1914. *Dallas Morning News.*

A Nazi government automobile that had driven into the river is being pulled out by German soldiers. Berlin, Germany, January 26, 1938. *New York Times*.

A ton of bricks, perhaps, fell on these new Chevys parked in a dealer's storage lot when a gasoline truck exploded while making a delivery to a close by garage on East 20th Street in New York City. October 3, 1949. *Collection of John Talbott.*

A Union Pacific freight train smashed into an empty school bus in a snowstorm. The wreckage draped over the cowcatcher like a shroud. Salt Lake City, Utah, December, 1938. *American Red Cross.*

Serious damage resulted when an express bus slammed into a concrete bridge pier on the New York Thruway near Oneida. The bus was speared by a guardrail. July 21, 1960. *Institute for Highway Safety.*

A teenage driver stopped his parents' Hudson on the tracks for a thrill. When the engineer of this locomotive of the Illinois Central's Panama Ltd. saw the car, he slammed on his brakes, derailing the locomotive and five passenger cars. The accident happened near Tangipahoa, Louisiana, May 18, 1930. The fifteen-year-old driver of the car was not injured. *Author's Collection.*

British Caledonian Railway O.6.O engine and tender are being hoisted back on track by two steam cranes and 174 railway men. The rolling stock slipped off the rails into a culvert after the land under the tracks fell away during winter rains. Date and location unknown. *National Rail Museum, York, UK.*

Vandals pushed this Alexandria, Virginia, schoolbus down a wooded ravine. January, 1972. *The Alexandria Gazette*.

When the wheels failed to lower, Eastern Airlines DC-7B landed safely in a grassy field rather than on the tarmac of the New Orleans, Louisiana Airport, January 15, 1959. *Savannah News*.

Both vehicles flipped when two saloon cars (what the English call sedans) smacked into each other at an intersection on Eshe Road near Liverpool. November 24, 1935. *The Benzinger Collection.*

A melancholy crowd looks on at an overturned laundry truck that was rammed on the flank by a meat truck in mid-town Chicago, Illinois, on September 9, 1946. *Chicago Times*.

A Bronx Park local on the New York Elevated Railroad ignored a signal and telescoped an empty early morning train at the 175th Street Station on the Third Avenue Line, on October 21, 1919. *Department of Cultural Affairs, State of Delaware.*

The driver was charged with reckless operation of this trolley, which overturned on the Eckington Line in Washington, D.C, September 5, 1921. *Robert Truax Collection*.

Attempting to make the first direct mail flight from Newark, New Jersey, to Palm Beach, Florida, transatlantic flyer Dick Merill ran into a bad storm. He brought the DC-2 down in the woods near Atamoras, Pennsylvania, by sliding in on her belly. One wing was torn off, but the fuselage held up well. December 19, 1936. *Air Museum.*

Hundreds of Douglas DC-3's have been used for military transport duty. This Army C-47 landed in a field near Woodbridge, Virginia, denting her nose and bashing the right engine. January, 1943. *Bureau of Aeronautics*.

The German freighter *Emstein* is badly gashed and sinking after sideswiping the Liberian freighter *Olympic Pearl*. The St. Clair River, near Courtright, Ontario, Canada, October 7, 1966. *Great Lakes Institute.*

This is the bow section of the Liberian oil tanker *Spartan Lady*, which split in two during angry weather. U.S. Coast Guard cannon fire sent what was left of her to the bottom of the Atlantic. One hundred miles southeast of Cape Cod, Massachusetts, April 4, 1975. *USCG*.

A fishing trawler is breaking up on the rocks at Point Augusta, Alaska. A crewman is being rescued by a breeches buoy. November 1, 1951. *Bureau of Navigation.*

National Transportation Safety Board

Annual Report
to Congress
1982

On January 13, 1982, an Air Florida Boeing 737 taking off from the Washington, D.C., National Airport crashed into a bridge during a snowstorm and plunged into the Potomac River. A portion of the plane's tail remained on the bridge. *NTSB.*

Curious Brits gather to look at the aftermath of a morning smashup of two Southern Railway electric commuter trains. They met head on in a fog at South Croyden, near London, October 24, 1947. *New York Times.*

The 7:33 A.M. LMS (London, Midland, and Scottish Railway) Express bound for Brimingham from Crewe derailed on a curve and crashed down an embankment. The engine was nearly embedded in the culvert. Investigators and work gangs begin the work of clearing the tracks. Great Bridgeford, England, June 18, 1932. *Author's Collection*.

Left: A messy accident occurred at Swanley near London, England. When the locomotive derailed, the first coach leapt over the locomotive; then the following cars smashed into the others. Wooden coaches offered little protection to the travelers. July 7, 1937. *British Rail.*

Below: The date and cause of this extraordinary pile up of freight cars is unknown. Menlo Park, California. *Smithsonian Institution.*

A smashup on U.S. route 301, La Plata, Maryland, badly damaged a Nash Ambassador Airflyte,
nicknamed "the bathtub" because of its fastback styling, 1950. *Bureau of Public Roads.*

Right: A 1941 Oldsmobile was rear-ended by a truck hauling
concrete blocks on the Virginia side of the 14th Street
Bridge just across the Potomac River from Washington,
D.C. The 10:45 A.M. wreck drew a crowd of military men
from the nearby Pentagon. September 8, 1950. *Bureau of
Public Roads.*

A Piper Cub made a nose dive into a farmer's field near Conway, Washington. Note the hay wagon and threshing equipment in the lefthand side of the background. August 23, 1946. *National Archives.*

A 5-ton truck piloted by James Fuller sideswiped a car, veered airborne from the raised highway and landed chin-on atop an 8-foot stone wall. Near Paoli, Pennsylvania, February 4, 1931. *New York Times*.

Trying to make a loop, but ending in a nosedive, the pilot of this army pursuit Curtis Warhawk P-40 smashed the plane's face in a field near Cold Bay, Alaska, October 7, 1942. *National Archives.*

J.T. Giles was trying to land at a local airport. Instead, he came down on the roof of a nearby house. La Grange, Georgia, December 24, 1949. *New York Times.*

A Mercury hit a heavy Hudson that crossed the double line in rural Iowa, 1949. *Bureau of Public Roads.*

A spring tornado ripped through a neighborhood in Greensboro, North Carolina, tearing into houses and tossing cars and trucks upside down. May, 1936. *American Red Cross*.

This messy pile-up of steel occurred when an Illinois Central freight train slipped off the rails at a curve near Monroe, Louisiana. The roadbed was weakened by a sudden winter thaw. January 18, 1929. *Author's Collection.*

Right: Tank cars were strewn in a zigzag near Cresson, Pennsylvania, after the engine exploded. November 14, 1942. *Pittsburgh Post.*

BIBLIOGRAPHY

Berman, Bruce D. *Encyclopedia of American Shipwrecks.*Boston, Mariner's Press, 1972.

Cornell, James. *The Great International Disaster Book.* New York: Scribners, 1976.

Cowan, Edward. *Oil and Water: The Torrey Canyon Disaster.* New York: Lippincott, 1968.

Deighton, Len. *Airshipwreck.* New York: Holt, 1978.

Eastlake, Keith. *Great Train Disaster.* Osceola: Motorbooks, 1997.

Eddy, Paul. *Destination Disaster.* New York: Quadrangle, 1976.

Fowles, John. *Shipwreck.* Boston: Little Brown, 1975.

Frank, Beryl. *Plane Crashes.* New York: Bell, 1981.

Gibbs, Jim. *Disaster Log of Ships.* Seattle: Superior, 1971.

Gill, Crispin. *The Wreck of the Torrey Canyon.* Newton Abbot: David and Charles, 1967.

Godson, John. *Unsafe At Any Height.* London: Anthony Blond, 1970.

Hoehling, A. A. *Great Ship Disasters.* New York: Cowles, 1971.

Johnson, George. *The Abominable Airlines.* New York: Macmillan, 1964.

Kaplan, H.R. *Voyager Beware.* New York: Rand McNally, 1966.

Kearney, Paul W. *Highway Homicide.* New York: Crowell, 1966.

McClement, Fred. *It Doesn't Matter Where You Sit.* New York: Holt, 1969.

Mielke, Otto. *Disaster At Sea.* New York: Fleet, 1958.

Morgan, Len. *Crackup.* New York: Arco, 1975.

Nader, Ralph. *Unsafe At Any Speed.* New York: Grossman, 1972.

Nash, Jay R. *Darkest Hours.* New York: Simon & Schuster, 1978.

O'Connell, Jeffrey. *Safety Last: An Indictment of the Auto Industry.* New York: Random House, 1966.

Perkes, Dan. *Eyewitness to Disaster.* Maplewood: Hammond, 1976.

Rolt, L. T. C. *Red for Danger.* London, Pan Books, 1966.

Schneider, Ascanio. *Railway Accidents of Great Britain.* Newton Abbot: David and Charles, 1968.

Shaw, Robert B. *Down Brakes.* London: Macmillan, 1961.

Winslow, Ron. *Hard Aground: Story of the Argo Merchant Oil Spill.* New York: Norton, 1978.